R{

St. Helens Libraries

Please return / renew this item by the last date shown.
Books may also be renewed by phone and Internet.
Telephone – (01744) 676954 or 677822
Email – centrallibrary@sthelens.gov.uk
Online – http://eps.sthelens.gov.uk/rooms

DEFENDER

Michael Hurley

www.raintreepublishers.co.uk
Visit our website to find out
more information about
Raintree books.

To order:
☎ Phone 0845 6044371
▤ Fax +44 (0) 1865 312263
▥ Email myorders@raintreepublishers.co.uk

Customers from outside the UK please telephone +44 1865 312262

Raintree is an imprint of Capstone Global Library Limited,
a company incorporated in England and Wales having its
registered office at 7 Pilgrim Street, London, EC4V 6LB
– Registered company number: 6695582

Edited by Louise Galpine, Vaarunika Dharmapala,
 and John-Paul Wilkins
Designed by Philippa Jenkins
Original illustrations © Capstone Global Library Ltd 2010
Illustrated by KJA-artists.com
Picture research by Hannah Taylor
Originated by Capstone Global Library Ltd
Printed and bound in China by Leo Paper Products Ltd

ISBN 978 1 406216 40 0 (hardback)
14 13 12 11 10
10 9 8 7 6 5 4 3 2 1

British Library Cataloguing in Publication Data
Hurley, Michael
Defender. -- (Football files)
796.3'342-dc22
A full catalogue record for this book is available
from the British Library.

Acknowledgements
We would like to thank the following for permission to
reproduce photographs: Action Images pp. **6**, **22** (John
Sibley), **24** (John Sibley); Corbis pp. **13** (Bettmann),
16 (Reuters/Alessandro Bianchi), **29** (Steve Woods); Getty
Images pp. **5** (Jamie McDonald), **7** (Ryan Pierse), **8** (Alex
Livesey), **20** (AFP/Odd Andersen), **23** (David Cannon),
27 (AFP/Andrew Yates); © KPT Power Photos **background
image**; Press Association pp. **10** (Empics/S&G and Barratts),
12 (AP Photo), **14** (Grazia Neri), **15** (Empics/Neal Simpson),
18 (PA Archive), **19** (Sean Dempsey); Shutterstock
background image (© Nikola I).

Cover photograph of Manchester United's Rio Ferdinand
(right) as he struggles for the ball with Liga de Quito's
Claudio Bieler during the final of the FIFA Club World
Cup, Yokohama, 21 December 2008, reproduced with
permission of Getty Images/AFP/Yoshikazu Tsuno.

We would like to thank Dr Sarah Schenker for her invaluable
help in the preparation of this book.

CONTENTS

Some words are shown in bold, **like this**. You can find out what they mean by looking in the glossary on page 30.

BEING A DEFENDER

More people play football than any other sport in the world. It is popular with people of all ages, races, and backgrounds. You do not need very much equipment to play a basic form of the game. If you don't have a football you can use a different kind of ball, or anything else that can be kicked around. Some people even play with tennis balls or old drinks cans.

Professional footballers get paid to play football. They play for teams in professional **leagues**. The leagues are organized by national football associations. If you are not a professional footballer you can still enjoy playing football for fun and exercise.

Organized football matches have two teams with eleven players on each side. Each team is made up of players who have different positions and roles on the pitch. A team will usually have four defenders. There will be two **centre-backs** and two **full-backs**, one of each on the left and the right of the pitch. The defenders work with the **goalkeeper** to make sure that the **opposition** does not score a goal.

You need certain skills to be a really good defender. Whether they are centre-backs or full-backs, all defenders need to be able to **tackle** well. They need to be alert and focused at all times during a match. Centre-backs are usually tall and strong. They must be good at **headers** and at **marking** the opposition players. Full-backs need to have **pace** and good **positioning**. They also need to be able to mark the opposition players.

Full-backs are often involved in attacking moves during a match. Tall centre-backs who are good at headers can be very useful for attacking moves such as **corners** and **free kicks**.

Manchester City's defender Wayne Bridge (right) battles for the ball with Richard Stearman of Wolverhampton Wanderers in an English Premier League match in 2009.

John Terry is a centre-back. He plays for Chelsea and England. Terry's career began at Chelsea when he was 14 years old. At first he was a **midfielder** but he soon changed his position to become a defender. He is very good at **headers** and **tackling**. He can pass accurately and he can score goals as well.

Playing for Chelsea

Terry made his **debut** for Chelsea in a **League** Cup match in 1998. He came off the **substitutes** bench during the match. Later in the season, Terry replaced an established **centre-back** on the team. This was the beginning of a very successful career.

John Terry (right) takes on Valerenga's Bjorn Levernes in the European Cup Winner's Cup quarter-final in 1999.

After **consistent** performances for Chelsea in the 2000/01 season, Terry was named the club's Player of the Year. In 2004 he was made the team captain. He is a leader on the pitch, and knows how to instruct and encourage his teammates.

Terry has become the most successful captain in Chelsea's history, winning seven major trophies, including two league titles and two FA Cups.

Playing for England

In 2005 Terry helped his team to win the league title for the first time in 50 years. The team also won the League Cup in the same year. In the next season, Chelsea successfully defended their league title. By this time, Terry had become a regular England international player. He made his debut as a substitute in 2003 and took part in his first full match for England in the same year. He played for England at the **UEFA** European Championships in 2004 and the World Cup in 2006. Terry was England captain between 2006 and 2010.

John Terry celebrates scoring a goal against Ukraine during a qualifying match for the 2010 World Cup.

Hitting the post

One of the biggest disappointments in Terry's career so far was the UEFA Champions League final in 2008. Chelsea lost against Manchester United in a **penalty shoot-out** after a thrilling match ended in a 1–1 draw. Terry had the chance to win the match for Chelsea but he slipped as he took his **penalty**. The ball hit the post. Terry was devastated and after the match he apologized to his teammates and fans. However, he did not let it affect his performances in the following season. He was just as committed as ever and helped his team to win the 2009 FA Cup.

John Terry misses a penalty against Manchester United in the Champions League final in 2008. Many great players have missed from the penalty spot.

Health and fitness

John Terry has a pasta meal at least three hours before a match to give his muscles the energy they need to last a whole game. Pasta is a carbohydrate, which is a type of food that releases energy into the body slowly. He has said, "The most successful teams win a lot of their games in the last 10 minutes. If you want to keep going for the full 90 and beyond, you need the right fuel inside you."

DEFENSIVE HEADER

John Terry is very good at headers. When he is defending, he tries to use his strength so that he can reach a ball in the air before the opposition does and head it clear. When he is attacking, he will try to time his run so that he can make contact with an approaching ball and head it towards the opposition's goal.

1. The ball is in the air and both the defender (in blue) and the attacker (in red) keep their eyes on it.

2. The defender jumps higher than her opponent and pushes her head forwards to meet the ball. She makes contact before the attacker can and clears the ball.

BOBBY MOORE

Bobby Moore was a **centre-back**. He signed his first **professional** contract with West Ham United on his 17th birthday. He played more than 500 times for West Ham, and was part of the team when they won the FA Cup in 1964. In the same season, he was given the English Footballer of the Year Award. He left West Ham in 1974 and joined Fulham. He also spent two years playing football in the United States before retiring in 1978.

Moore was not tall for a centre-back but he was able to **anticipate** what would happen during a match. He used this skill to get to the ball before an **opponent** could. Moore was respected by both his teammates and his opponents. He was known for his honesty, loyalty, and calm, both on and off the pitch.

Bobby Moore (left) and West Ham United teammate Ken Brown help each other to clear the ball.

Health and fitness

In Moore's day, players knew very little about nutrition and would often sit down to a fried breakfast together. These days, players avoid fatty foods and eat cereals, wholegrains, yoghurts, and fruit for breakfast. They know that eating the right foods helps them to train and play to the best of their ability.

ACCURATE PASSING

It is important for defenders to be able to pass accurately to a teammate in order to keep possession of the ball for their team. Bobby Moore was well-known for his accurate passing.

1. Stand over the ball with one foot beside it and the other ready to swing.

2. Swing to make contact with the middle of the ball, using the inside of your foot.

3. Keep your eyes on the ball as you make the pass. This is a sidefoot pass, which is very accurate because so much of your boot is touching the ball.

World Cup 1966

Moore was an England international. He made over 100 appearances for his country, including 90 as captain. One of the greatest moments in Moore's career was the World Cup in 1966, which was held in England. The England team were expected to do well in the tournament. Moore helped his team to the final, where they played West Germany. England were leading 2–1 until the final few minutes of the game when West Germany scored to draw level.

Bobby Moore and Brazil's Pelé exchange shirts after a World Cup match in 1970.

Moore's influence and calm approach helped England to keep going in **extra-time**. England managed to make the score 3–2. After nearly 120 minutes of football Moore showed what a great player he was. He received the ball just outside the England **penalty** area. He played a long pass to one of his teammates, Geoff Hurst. Hurst took control of the ball, ran forward, and shot at the West German goal. He scored. England won the match 4–2 and became World Cup winners. Moore was presented with the winner's trophy by the Queen.

Bobby Moore holds up the World Cup trophy as he celebrates victory with his England teammates in 1966.

Services to football

In 1967 Moore was awarded an OBE (Order of the British Empire) by the Queen for his services to football. After a lifetime of achievement, Moore died of cancer in 1993. When he died, the famous Brazilian footballer Pelé said, "He was my friend as well as the greatest defender I ever played against."

PAOLO MALDINI

Paolo Maldini played **professionally** for 25 years. He joined his local team, AC Milan, when he was 10 years old. His father, Cesare, had played for Milan during his own successful football career. Maldini made his **debut** for AC Milan when he was just 16 years old. He came off the **substitutes** bench in the second half of a **league** match against Udinese in Serie A (the Italian League).

Here, Paolo Maldini is in action for AC Milan on his debut in 1985.

Playing for AC Milan

Maldini made over 900 appearances for AC Milan and never played for any other club. He said, "I'm proud to have been at this club since I was 10. For someone born and bred in this city, playing for Milan is very special." At AC Milan he played with great stars such as Franco Baresi, Ruud Gullit, and Kaka. Maldini played as a **left-back** for most of his career. He used his good **positioning** skills to make **interceptions** and **tackles** against the **opposition**. He was also a terrific leader, and was captain of AC Milan and Italy during his career.

Paolo Maldini (left) times his tackle just right while playing for Italy against Croatia in 2002.

Record breaker!

Paolo Maldini is the second most **capped** player in Italian football history. He made 126 appearances for Italy before retiring from international football in 2002.

Paolo Maldini raises the Champions League trophy after AC Milan's victory over Juventus in 2003.

While Maldini was at AC Milan the team enjoyed great success. They won the Serie A title seven times and they made it to eight **UEFA** Champions League finals. Maldini played in each one of these eight finals. In 2003 he was the captain when Milan beat their fierce rivals Juventus in the final, on penalties. Maldini won the trophy five times with AC Milan. The first time was in 1989 and the last time was in 2007.

Beating Liverpool

Two years later he was involved in one of the most famous finals in recent history. AC Milan were playing Liverpool. One minute into the match Maldini scored a **header**. By half-time, AC Milan were 3–0 up. In the second half Liverpool staged a magnificent fightback, managing to level the score at 3–3. Once again, the match ended with penalties. This time Milan lost. It was heartbreaking for Maldini and his teammates. However, the team managed to get revenge for this defeat two years later. They played Liverpool again in the Champions League final in 2007. This time Milan won the match 2–1.

Health and fitness

As he got older Maldini lost some of his **pace**. He changed his position from left-back to centre-back, where pace is not as important. In recent years, players have been able to continue playing top-level football as they get older. This is because of improvements in diet and fitness.

MAN MARKING

Maldini was very good at **anticipating** what would happen next in a match. He would stay close to the opposition **striker** and watch his every move. This is called man **marking**. If the ball came near the striker, Maldini could capture the ball. There is also another type of marking called zonal marking. Players will defend an area of the pitch rather than a single **opponent**.

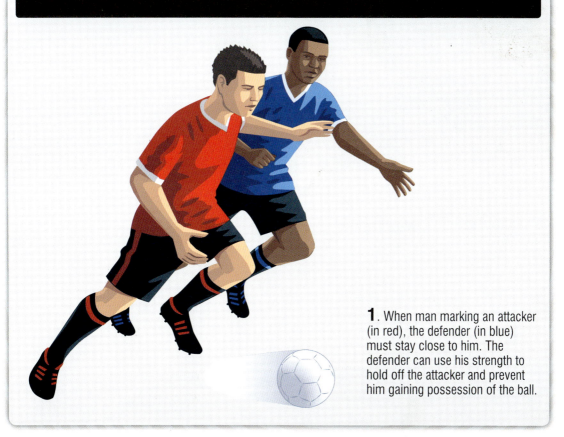

1. When man marking an attacker (in red), the defender (in blue) must stay close to him. The defender can use his strength to hold off the attacker and prevent him gaining possession of the ball.

RIO FERDINAND

Rio Ferdinand is a Manchester United and England **centre-back**. Since joining Manchester United in 2002 he has won the **league** four times, the League Cup twice, and the **UEFA** Champions League once.

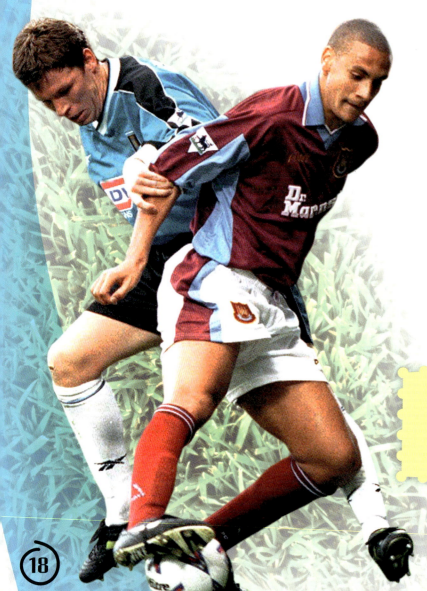

Ferdinand grew up in a poor area of London. He began playing football in the local streets as a young child. He has a famous uncle, Les Ferdinand, who was a **professional** footballer and Rio wanted to be one as well. He had to work hard. He had to train and practise all the time to become one of the best defenders in the world.

Rio Ferdinand (right) uses his strength to challenge an opponent during an English Premier League match.

Playing for West Ham United and England

Ferdinand joined West Ham United in 1992. He stood out as a young defender. Along with good **tackling** and **heading** ability, Ferdinand was very good at passing. He also had the ability to begin attacking moves by bringing the ball out of defence with confidence. Ferdinand made his West Ham **debut** in a league match at the end of the 1995/96 season. In the next season he was regularly included in the starting line-up.

Ferdinand's skilful and **consistent** performances in the Premier League meant that he was called up to the England team. He made his international debut in a match against Cameroon in 1997 and was made captain in 2010.

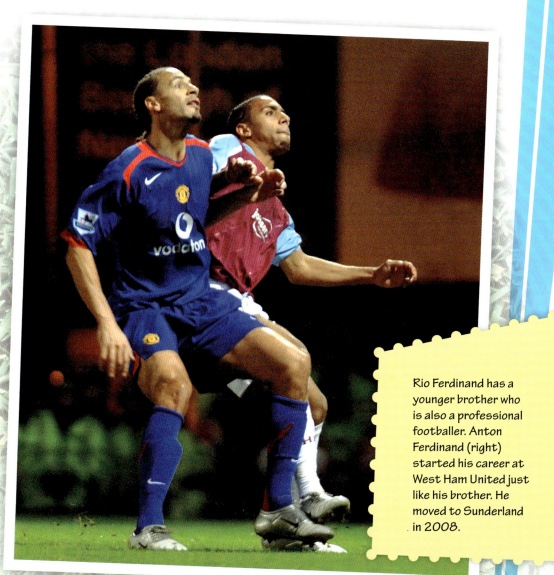

Rio Ferdinand has a younger brother who is also a professional footballer. Anton Ferdinand (right) started his career at West Ham United just like his brother. He moved to Sunderland in 2008.

Playing for Leeds and Manchester United

After 158 appearances for West Ham United, Ferdinand was signed by Leeds United for £18 million. He joined an exciting young team who were competing in the Premier League and Champions League. After a short spell with Leeds, Ferdinand transferred to Manchester United in 2002. Manchester United paid £30 million for him, smashing the world record for a defender. Ferdinand

played 28 matches in the league in his first season. He helped Manchester United to win the league. It was a great start to his career at his new club.

In 2003, Ferdinand missed a drugs test and, as punishment, was banned from playing for eight months. He missed the last few months of the season with Manchester United, as well as the chance to play for England at the 2004 UEFA European Championships.

Rio Ferdinand (right) heads the ball away from Portugal's Pauleta during the World Cup quarter-final in 2006.

Manchester United won the Premier League three years in a row, from 2006 to 2009. Ferdinand was an important part of the team during this time. In 2008 the team made it to the UEFA Champions League final. They won the match after a **penalty shoot-out**. One year later they made it to the final again. This time Manchester United were outplayed by a brilliant Barcelona team, and beaten 2–0. Ferdinand will try to help his club team and England win many more trophies before he retires.

TACKLING

All defenders need to be able to tackle well. **Opposition** players do not often get past Rio Ferdinand with the ball. If they do, he is quick enough to catch them and tackle them.

1. Two players approach the ball.

2. The defender (in blue) moves towards his opponent, keeping his eyes on the ball. He is preparing to tackle his opponent using the inside of his foot.

3. The defender's aim is to win possession of the ball without fouling the opposition player. This is known as a clean tackle.

Racism in football

Unfortunately racism is still sometimes a part of football. When England played Spain in a friendly match in 2004, some of the Spanish supporters targeted black English players like Rio Ferdinand and Ashley Cole. They made it clear that they did not like the players because of their skin colour. They chanted and made noises.

The players tried to ignore what was happening but after the match they asked for something to be done. UEFA fined the Spanish FA and made it clear that this type of behaviour is totally unacceptable. It is now only a very small percentage of supporters who do this sort of thing. Hopefully in the future it will not happen at all.

ROBERTO CARLOS

Roberto Carlos da Silva is one of the most famous and successful **left-backs** to have ever played football. He is not a typical left-back because although he has good defensive skills, he is most effective when he is attacking. He is famous for running down the left wing and using his **pace** and strength to set up attacking moves for his team. Like most Brazilian players, he has very good **technique**.

Roberto Carlos' football career began with his local team União São João, in Brazil. He became a **professional** at the age of 20 when he signed his first contract with Palmeiras, a famous Brazilian club team. Roberto Carlos made 68 appearances for Palmeiras in two years. He was signed by Italian giants Internazionale (Inter Milan) in 1995. He spent only one season at Internazionale. He impressed many people with his determined performances for the team.

Here, Roberto Carlos is in action for Internazionale in 1995.

In demand

Roberto Carlos played well enough in his year with Internazionale for Brazil to include him in their squad for the 1996 Olympics. Brazil finished third in the competition. After the Olympics, Roberto Carlos joined Spain's Real Madrid. He went on to play in 370 league matches with them, scoring 47 goals, an amazing achievement for a defender. He was part of the Real Madrid team that won the Champions **League** in 1998, 2000, and 2002. He also won the Spanish league title four times while at Real Madrid. After eleven seasons Roberto Carlos left Madrid and joined Fenerbahce in Turkey on a two-year contract in 2007. In 2009 he moved back to Brazil, to join Corinthians.

Carlos has made 125 appearances for Brazil during his career. He has scored 19 goals. He was an important member of the Brazil team that won the World Cup in 2002. He said, "Taking part in the World Cup is the most important thing that has happened in my life. It's every player's dream."

Roberto Carlos (middle) cradles the World Cup after helping Brazil to win the tournament in 2002.

Free kicks

Carlos is probably best known for his powerful shooting, especially his free kicks. His power and accuracy when striking a football is amazing. He can shoot from anywhere in the opponent's half. He has scored some outstanding goals. His skill and technique mean that he is very useful to his team when taking **corners** and **free kicks**.

Roberto Carlos strikes one of his powerful free kicks in a match against Juventus in 2003.

Power and strength

Roberto Carlos is thought to have one of the most powerful shots in the world at 137 kilometres per hour (85 miles per hour).

SLIDING TACKLE

Sometimes you need to slide across the pitch to make a tackle. This is called a **sliding tackle**. Roberto Carlos often uses his strength and pace to help him make sliding tackles. To be as successful as him, you need to time the tackle well. If you get your timing wrong you may commit a foul. This would give a free kick to the **opposition**.

1. Two players approach the ball.

2. The defender (in blue) tackles from the side and slides across the path of his opponent.

3. By timing the tackle well, the defender has won the ball. He is able to move away from his opponent with the ball.

TIPS FOR DEFENDERS

Tackling

All defenders must be able to **tackle** well. It is one of the most important skills for a defender. When making a tackle, keep your eyes on the ball, try to stay on your feet, and make sure you get your timing right.

Heading

All defenders, but especially **centre-backs**, need to be good at heading the ball. When making a defensive **header**, keep your eyes on the ball and try to time your jump so that your forehead makes contact with the ball at the peak of the jump. If you close your eyes before you head the ball it may not go where you want it to!

Marking and intercepting

It is important to stay between your **opponents** and the goal. Try to **anticipate** when your direct opponent is going to receive the ball. You can follow them and try to capture the ball when it comes near. If you do not concentrate, you could lose the player you are **marking**.

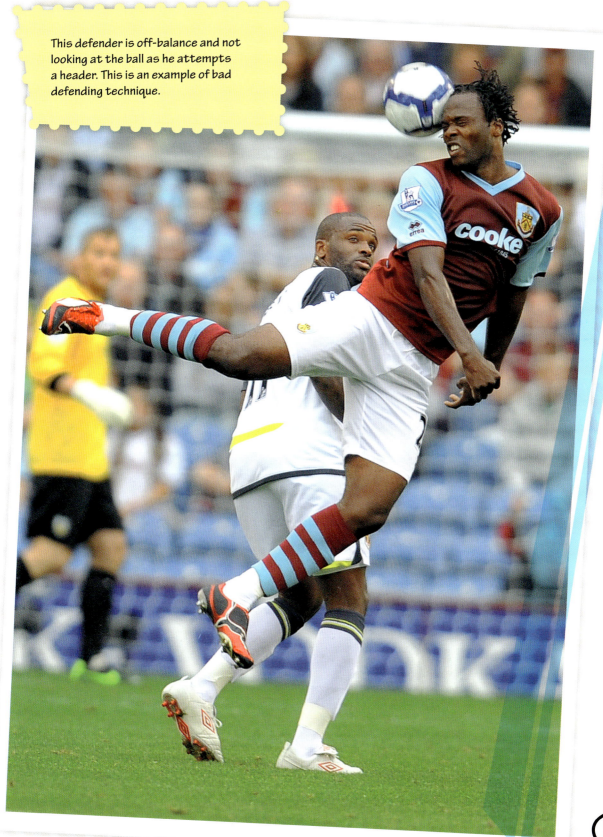

This defender is off-balance and not looking at the ball as he attempts a header. This is an example of bad defending technique.

Short-range passing

Passing over a short distance to a teammate means that your team is more likely to keep possession of the ball. When passing over a short distance, make sure that you keep your eyes on the ball as you kick it. If you use the inside of your foot (see page 11) you will have more control over the direction and **pace** of the pass.

Organization and communication

Communication between the defenders and their **goalkeeper** is very important. The goalkeeper can help the defenders to stay focused and organized during a match. He can shout instructions about where to go and who to mark. Remember that the goalkeeper can see more than you can because he is behind you on the pitch.

Long-range passing

It can be important for defenders to be able to pass the ball to a teammate who is further up the pitch. When passing over a long distance you must make sure that you judge the speed of your pass so that it reaches a teammate. If you are not accurate with your passing your team will lose possession of the ball.

This defender is using his strength to hold off his opponent.

GLOSSARY

anticipate perform before another player has a chance to react

capped each time a player makes an appearance for their national team they are given a cap

centre-back position of a player on the pitch. A centre-back is a defender who plays in the centre of defence.

consistent always the same

corner kick taken by the attacking team from the corner of the pitch after the defending team has knocked the ball over the goal line

cross kicking the ball from one side of the pitch to a player in the middle, usually near the goal

debut first time that a player plays for a team

extra-time extra period of play that is added on to some football matches if there is a draw after 90 minutes. Extra time lasts for 30 minutes, with two halves of 15 minutes.

free kick kick of the ball awarded by the referee after a foul

full-back position of a player on the pitch. A full-back is a defender who plays as either a right- or left-sided defender.

goalkeeper position of a player on the pitch. The goalkeeper guards the goal and is the only player allowed to touch the ball with his hands.

header when you connect with the ball using your head

interception getting to the ball before an opposition player

league group of teams that play against each other during the football season. There are national football leagues all over the world.

left-back position of a player on the pitch. A left-back plays as the left full-back.

mark keep close to an opponent to try to stop them getting the ball

midfielder position of a player on the pitch. Midfielders link the attacking and defending players.

opponent/opposition person or team that you are playing against

pace speed. A player with lots of pace can move around the pitch quickly.

penalty the referee gives a penalty if a foul happens in the 18-yard box. The ball is placed on a spot 12 yards (10.9 metres) from the goal and only the goalkeeper is allowed to stop the shot.

penalty shoot-out if the scores are level after extra time five players from each team try to score a penalty each. The team that scores the most penalties wins.

positioning placing yourself in a good position in relation to the ball and your opponents

professional being paid to do something. Professional footballers earn a salary for playing football.

sliding tackle take the ball away from an opponent by sliding on the ground and using the feet or legs to block and hold the ball

striker position of a player on the pitch. Strikers try to score goals.

substitute players who do not start a match but who can replace a player on the pitch. Three substitutes can be used in most matches.

tackle take the ball from an opponent using your feet

technique way of doing something. Different players control the ball in different ways on the pitch, and there is good and bad technique for certain passes and skills.

UEFA (Union of European Football Associations) organization responsible for European football

FIND OUT MORE

Books to read

Usborne Activities: 50 Soccer Skills, Jonathan Sheikh-Miller (Usborne, 2008)

Essential Sports: Football, Andy Smith (Heinemann Library, 2008)

Skills (Know the Game): Soccer – Defending (A&C Black, 2007)

Sport Files: Wayne Rooney, John Townsend (Raintree, 2009)

The World Cup series, Michael Hurley (Heinemann Library, 2009)

Websites

http://www.thefa.com/skills

The website of the English Football Association. This site has lots of videos to help you improve your skills and technique.

http://news.bbc.co.uk/sport2/hi/academy/default.stm

The BBC Sport Academy website includes videos and tutorials to help you learn more about playing football.

http://www.fifa.com/aboutfifa/developing/medical/playerhealth.html

The FIFA website has information about how to get the most out of playing football by eating healthily and avoiding injuries.

INDEX